D1523466

Young Heroes

Hannah Taylor
Helping the Homeless

Q.L. Pearce

KIDHAVEN PRESS
A part of Gale, Cengage Learning

GALE
CENGAGE Learning™

Detroit • New York • San Francisco • New Haven, Conn • Waterville, Maine • London

GALE
CENGAGE Learning™

LIBRARY OF CONGRESS CATALOGING-IN-PUBLICATION DATA

Pearce, Q.L. (Querida Lee)
  Hannah Taylor : helping the homeless / Q.L. Pearce.
    p. cm. — (Young heroes)
  Includes bibliographical references and index.
  ISBN 978-0-7377-4051-6 (hardcover)
  1. Taylor, Hannah, 1996– 2. Social reformers—Canada—Biography—Juvenile literature. 3. Philanthropists—Canada—Biography—Juvenile literature. 4. Ladybug Foundation—Juvenile literature. 5. Homelessness—Canada—Juvenile literature. I. Title.
  HV4509.P43 2008
  362.5′57632092—dc22
  [B]   2008011146

KidHaven Press
27500 Drake Rd.
Farmington Hills, MI 48331

ISBN-13: 978-0-7377-4051-6
ISBN-10: 0-7377-4051-5

Printed in the United States of America
2 3 4 5 6 7 12 11 10 09 08

Contents

Chapter One:
A Kind Heart 4

Chapter Two:
Sad Hearts in Old Clothes 11

Chapter Three:
The Ladybug Foundation 19

Chapter Four:
A Message of Hope 28

Notes 37
Glossary 40
For Further Exploration 42
Index. 45
Picture Credits 47
About the Author 48

A Kind Heart

At the age of five, Hannah Taylor saw a man eating food from a garbage can. She could not forget that image and vowed to help change the conditions that had led to his **plight.**

Hannah came up with a plan to raise money to help the homeless. She soon established the Ladybug Foundation, an organization devoted to this goal. Hannah does much more than raise money. She travels throughout her Canadian homeland and beyond presenting the message that the homeless are ordinary people dealing with very difficult times. They deserve to be treated with **dignity.** At the age of eleven, Hannah was presented with the 2007 Brick Award for Community Building for her extraordinary efforts, and she has been named as one of Canada's most powerful women.

She continues to work toward her goal, setting an example with her love and **dedication** as expressed in her open letter to the homeless: "Hello to all my friends from around the world who are lost, alone, hungry and homeless. My Name is Hannah Taylor, and even though I might not know all of your names—I want you to know I care."[1]

Hannah at Home

Hannah Catherine Taylor was born in Winnipeg, Manitoba, Canada, on January 18, 1996. She is the third in a family of four children. Her older brother and sister are both in college. Hannah's brother, Quinn, studies finance, and her sister, Hilary, is a science student. Her little sister, Gabriella, is five years younger than Hannah and is "very smart and stubborn."[2]

Hannah's dad, Bruce Taylor, is a lawyer with a great sense of humor. Her mother, Colleen Taylor, a former nurse, is a full-time mom who regularly volunteers at the Ladybug Foundation. Colleen has a special nickname for Hannah. She often calls her "Tiger Lily" after the loyal, strong-willed character in *Peter Pan* who was not afraid to stand up for a friend even when it was not easy.

The family also includes two dachshund dogs named Bella and Abigail, a large blue fish named Natalia, and a kitty named Charlotte. "Bella and Charlotte are best friends. They do not see their differences. They just feel with their hearts, and that is how I wish it always was,"[3] Hannah says.

The Taylor family is very close, and they enjoy doing things together. They often go to a nearby lake to hike, or they hang around together reading, listening to music, or enjoying a movie night. Recently they worked together on a project called Homes of Hope. The family traveled to Mexico, where they helped to build a house

Hannah (bottom right) takes a moment from her charity work to spend time with her family.

for a homeless family. "We loved this family, and my mom cried a lot," Hannah explains. "But she finally stopped when we got the house done."[4]

Hannah's favorite place to visit is her grandparents' cottage, where she often spends her summers. She takes advantage of the opportunity to explore nature and share special time with her "Nana and Papa."[5] Hannah explains that although her grandmother's eyesight is poor, she is very active and is an excellent cook. "Nana is the best cook in the world, and she has the biggest, most beautiful heart ever," Hannah says with enthusiasm. "She is my hero because she taught me that you can do anything if you just set your heart to it and work hard and believe."[6]

Pastimes and School Days

At home in Winnipeg, one of Hannah's preferred pastimes is reading. She looks forward to trips to the local bookstore and to a special antique store that carries old books and other treasures. "I love old things because they have a story. I just stand in that antique store and imagine all the stories attached to every single thing in there,"[7] Hannah explains. She is also fond of dragons, writing, drawing, and music. Hannah plays the flute and the guitar, and she sings in a choir. Several sports are on her list of passions, including basketball, horseback riding, and swimming. She is a member of a team in the sport of ultimate, a game played with a flying disc.

Hannah attends St. John's-Ravenscourt School. It is one of Canada's leading independent university-preparatory schools, with roots in the community that can be traced to the early 1800s. She describes it as a place that really makes you want to learn. Although she enjoys all of her subjects, her favorite is language arts. During her free time, Hannah says simply that she and her friends hang around together and talk and laugh a lot. "Sometimes we watch movies and eat junk. My friends and I do sleepover parties, but I get homesick, so I have a hard time sleeping away from home. But this year I did two sleepover camps for school and choir and I did okay."[8]

A Sad Reality

A great deal of Hannah's time is devoted to her work of helping the homeless. Her **commitment** to this issue began when she was only five years old. While driving, Hannah's mom turned down a back lane, where they saw a **disheveled** man eating out of a garbage can. "I asked my mom what he was doing, and why he was doing it, because it was the first time I had ever seen a homeless person," Hannah says. "She gently told me that the man was homeless, and they do what they have to do to eat."[9]

Hannah could not forget about the unfortunate man. She could not understand why some people had to live without enough food or proper shelter. During Winnipeg's long, cold winters, temperatures may dip as low as -45°F (-43°C). Hannah continued to ask her mom about homelessness. She reasoned that if everyone shared what he or she had, the problem could be solved. When she saw another homeless person, a woman who carried everything she owned in a single

Hannah began helping the homeless, such as this man, when she was just five years old.

grocery cart, Hannah was heartbroken. Uncertain about how to help, she worried about the **dilemma** until her mother finally told her, "Well Hannah, maybe if you do something about it, maybe your heart will not feel so bad."[10]

Taking her mom's advice, Hannah asked her first-grade teacher if she could talk to the class about homelessness. When they heard what she had to say, her classmates agreed that they all had to do something to help. The result was a class bake sale. Families donated dozens of homemade treats, including pies, cakes, cupcakes, and cookies. The sale was a huge success, raising about five hundred dollars. All of the proceeds, as well as additional donations of clothing and blankets, went to a local mission.

Hannah spent the next year learning more about the issue of homelessness. By the time she was seven she had come up with a plan. She says, "I just thought if people knew about hunger and homelessness they would want to help and care however they could. I started to speak to big people, little people, and everyone in between."[11]

Chapter Two

Sad Hearts in Old Clothes

Hannah learned that few countries are able to give an accurate count of their homeless population, though the numbers may be in the many thousands. One reason is that people often move from place to place in search of shelter or an opportunity to find work. Sometimes they hide from society. Whole families may live in a car, embarrassed to let others know about their situation. According to the Ladybug Foundation Web site, twenty years ago the greatest number of homeless people were older men. Now they are more commonly men of the average age of twenty-nine.

There are many reasons why people may find themselves homeless. Sometimes it is about money. Some lose their jobs and their homes because of a change in the economy. Some have no permanent place because their jobs are seasonal, or they are recent **immigrants** who have

11

not found work. They may be elderly people with little income.

Sometimes there are other factors. People may become homeless because of mental health **disabilities** or drug or alcohol problems. The homeless also include children. Young people who run away, or abused women with small children, may find themselves living in shabby hotel rooms or without any shelter, proper meals, or medical care. Once someone is in a situation like this, it is hard to recover. It is difficult to apply for a job or enroll children in school without a permanent address.

A homeless woman and her son in their room in a shelter. Hannah found that children are a growing group of the homeless.

Hannah quickly recognized that the general public must understand that the homeless are people too. They deserve to be treated with dignity, but more importantly, they are not invisible. It only makes the issue worse when people turn away and pretend that the homeless are a problem that someone else must solve. Hannah hopes that people will "see them as members of their community, rather than as threats or as someone to avoid contact with or to outright ignore."[12] She believes that they are "great people wrapped in old clothes with sad hearts."[13] Hannah considers homeless and hungry people her heroes because of how hard they have to work simply to get through each day.

Meeting Rick Adams

In February 2003, at the age of seven, Hannah met Rick Adams at the Siloam Mission in Winnipeg. She describes him as a beautiful person. "My grown-up friend Julie introduced us at a shelter he went to for food and love,"[14] she says. When they met, Hannah gave him a hug and he began to cry. He said they were happy tears because Hannah was looking at him and talking to him. Adams was not used to being treated so kindly. Hannah **inspired** Adams. Because she cared about him, he began to take better care of himself. She has a picture of the two of them together. He wore his best shirt the day they took the picture.

Hannah recently had some great news from Rick Adams. He has found a job and has a home. She beams with happiness when she says, "Rick did it!! He showed me that kindness, hard work and caring from

Hannah being photographed with Rick Adams.

all of us—gives people hope. 'And when you have hope in your heart, all things are possible.'"[15] She adds, "I take Rick in my heart everywhere I go every time I speak about hunger, homelessness, and poverty. He is one of the reasons I do what I do."[16]

Part of what Hannah does to help her friends is raise money. She began with ladybug jars. Once, when shopping with her mom, she saw donation collection jars in stores. A jar was often placed near the checkout area where people could toss in their extra change to benefit a good cause. Hannah's little sister was a baby at the time, so there were plenty of baby food jars at home. Hannah had already decided to use a ladybug as her mascot because they are good luck. "And we all need that,"[17] Hannah says. She collected the small baby food jars, painted them red, and painted a ladybug on the top and dots on the sides. She made a hangtag telling people how to help.

The jars were cute enough to attract attention. Hannah loved seeing her idea take shape. There was one problem, though. "We accidentally did not realize that red spray paint floats in the air," she admits. "So my dad's car was kind of pinky red on one side until he traded it in."[18] Her father did not complain, and Hannah handed out the first 150 ladybug jars on her dad's birthday.

"Make Change" Month

The jars were a big hit, and people filled them with change to help the homeless. The roots of the Ladybug Foundation had been planted. Before long, generous

Hannah with a group of her ladybug jars for the homeless. The jars were a big hit and led to the creation of the Ladybug Foundation.

volunteers offered their time and creativity to help the foundation grow.

Canadian pop-rock singer-songwriter Chantal Kreviazuk contacted Colleen Taylor with an idea. She had been thinking about how Hannah wanted to make change for her ladybug jars, but what Hannah really wanted was to "Make Change" in the way the world sees hunger and homelessness. Hannah says, "So my Mom told me [about the idea], and I said, yes, we must 'Make Change,' and that was that."[19]

The idea led to "Make Change" Month. That is when the Ladybug Foundation gives ladybug jars to businesses and schools that request them. People fill the jars with spare change that will help to make a change in society. "The idea of someone as young as Hannah seeing the need to provide sanctuary for the homeless and her **conviction** that she can make a difference is just awesome," Chantal Kreviazuk says. "Hannah and the Ladybug Foundation's efforts to provide shelter for homeless people in Canada have been a real inspiration for me and I'm proud to be involved in any way."[20]

"Big Boss" Lunches

When Hannah was little she thought that her father was a big boss who made the important decisions for everyone. As she grew older, she found out that, like her father, many businesspeople make important decisions every day. She decided that if she could take some of these "big bosses" to lunch and talk to them about hunger and homelessness, they might help. She began by meeting with business leaders one at a time.

Hannah often meets with business and political leaders to speak about the homeless. Here, she is pictured with the Canadian minister of health Stephan Fletcher (far left), the Canadian prime minister Stephen Harper (far right), and her father Bruce (middle left).

Hannah says, "One day I came home a little **frustrated** because I thought it was taking too long this way, so I told my Mom maybe we could get all the big bosses together for a sandwich and some juice and I could talk to them all at once." Once the arrangements had been made, Hannah painted fifty special ladybug pictures and offered them for sale at her first Big Boss Lunch.

After telling her guests about homelessness, she showed them the paintings she had done to raise money. "One of the big bosses stood up after I spoke and asked me 'how much are your paintings Hannah.' I said 'let your heart decide,' and he bought one for ten thousand dollars and then everyone started to do the same. It was a great day!"[21]

Hannah now holds luncheons every year in major cities throughout Canada. Sometimes the foundation sells red fleece ladybug scarves and bracelets that read "Make Change." Hannah never loses sight of her purpose. She is there to give her guests an important message and to ask for their help. "I have learned that every three seconds someone dies because they don't have what I have,"[22] she once told a gathering of business leaders at the historic Fairmont Royal York Hotel in downtown Toronto.

Chapter Three

The Ladybug Foundation

Hannah encountered few roadblocks as she found new ways to help her homeless friends. She met great people who were willing to work hard. Her belief is that caring for each other makes our world better for everyone, not just the hungry and the homeless. "Everyone from the prime minister to school kids and big bosses and old and young people have helped and shared and volunteered, and that is how come we can have the Ladybug Foundation," Hannah explains. "It is completely run by volunteers, and everything is donated, even our office!"[23]

The Ladybug Foundation is a nonprofit **charitable** foundation. It was established in May 2004 to help support Hannah as she spreads her message of hope and teaches children and adults what they can do to help the

Hannah posing in front of a sponsor's cement truck painted with the Ladybug Foundation logo.

homeless. The foundation also aids fund-raising through special programs. These include **sponsorship** and **donor** campaigns for large companies and organizations.

According to its Web site, the foundation raises money to help charitable organizations that provide food, shelter, and other needs of the homeless in cities across Canada. The funds are given without strings and without judgment, so that the person in need is treated with dignity, safety, and hope.

Spreading the Word

Hannah is the voice of the foundation, and she writes her own speeches. Since May 2004, she has spoken to more than 150 schools, businesses, churches, government organizations, and other groups. Her message has appeared in newspapers and magazines, and she has been a guest on many radio and television shows.

In 2006 Hannah visited the Ecole Greenview School in Edmonton. "The response from our students was overwhelming," says fourth-grade teacher Lynda Horvath.

> Very soon, we saw examples of students starting to think about ways they could help others, in a new and "real" way. We saw a different attitude between the children in the classrooms and on the playground. They seemed to be more **tolerable** of each other, more **compassionate** and caring toward each other, especially on the playground.[24]

When searching for inspiration, Hannah thinks of the caring people who work at the shelters. She remembers the homeless and hungry who must do everything they can just to get through the day. She also counts the Dalai Lama among her inspirations. He is the spiritual leader of the people of Tibet. She particularly loves his quote: "It is time to begin educating the heart."[25] Those words have a special place on the wall at the Ladybug Foundation office.

Civil rights leader Martin Luther King Jr. also inspires Hannah because he believed and worked for what was right. She feels that he touched on a great truth when he said, "In the end we will not remember the words of our enemies but the silence of our friends."[26] Hannah says she believes that with all her heart.

"Homeless and hungry people are my friends, and I just cannot be silent about them ever, and I never will be."[27]

Audiences as large as 16,000 have gathered to hear Hannah speak. Spectators are amazed by Hannah's courage and confidence. "I do not get nervous. I just feel lucky that people come to listen," Hannah says. "Sometimes people cry a little because I think the topic makes their heart sadden and then they listen and clap and help."[28]

She is not discouraged when people are not interested and do not seem to care. She understands that people

Hannah gives a speech at a school about the Ladybug Foundation and homelessness.

have their own minds and do as they like. When asked what she feels the homeless want everyone to know, Hannah says that they want others to know that they are people. They have feelings, they had or have mothers and family, and that a homeless life was never what they wished for. "No one says, 'I want to be homeless when I grow up,'"[29] Hannah adds.

She has no problem speaking to well-known adults, such as celebrated **primatologist** Jane Goodall, who told Hannah about the problems of homeless children in Kenya, Africa. Hannah has even chatted with the political leaders of Canada. When she was seven years old, Prime Minister Paul Martin visited Winnipeg to give a speech. The organizers asked her to come and accept a donation for her cause. When Hannah learned that the event would be like a Big Boss Lunch, she asked her mom if she could give her speech. Colleen Taylor said no, but Hannah was so **persistent** that her mom finally telephoned Martin's office. They phoned back forty minutes later with an invitation from Martin himself. The current prime minister, Stephen Harper, sent Hannah a letter, too.

Time Management

Hannah admits that her schedule can be a challenge. She gives major speeches about three times a month, and there are plenty of other things to do for the Ladybug Foundation. Her teachers at school are supportive. However, she still has to keep up with her homework. "To be honest, I do not miss as much school as I would like to," Hannah admits. "But

When traveling for the Ladybug Foundation, Hannah misses her little sister Gabriella.

when I do miss school, I get the work that I am going to miss done before I leave."[30]

On a school day, Hannah might give a talk at a conference in the morning, go to classes in the afternoon, then return home and do homework in the evening. For a full Ladybug Foundation day, she usually flies to the location the night before, gives her speech that day, and flies out that night. When Hannah travels, either her mom or her dad goes with her, but she still gets homesick. "I miss my little sister. And each parent does not come with me. It is usually one or the other,"[31] she explains.

Extended Family

In April 2007, Hannah's travels took her and her family far from their home in Canada to Mariefred, Sweden. There she took her place as the youngest **jury** member to work with the World's Children's Prize for the Rights of the Child. Among the **patrons** of the group are Queen Silvia of Sweden and Nelson Mandela of South Africa.

Each year, a jury of fifteen children from around the world work together to select a person or organization to receive the World's Children's Prize for outstanding effort on behalf of children. Some of the jury members are former **refugees, debt slaves,** or victims of other rights abuses. Hannah's roommate in Sweden, Gaba, is an AIDS orphan from South Africa who works with other AIDS orphans. Thomas, a jury member from Uganda, was forced to be a child soldier. On the jury, Hannah represents "children fighting for other children's rights, especially the homeless children."[32]

She quickly grew to love and respect her new friends. When she returned home, saying good-bye to them was very hard. Hannah says:

> I bought a big map in Sweden and I got each one of my friends to put their handprint on the map and draw a heart around their home, and I have fourteen brave, beautiful-hearted friends' handprints hanging on the wall of the Ladybug Foundation office. When I watch the news or read the paper, I worry about them all, but I know they are strong and good and I cannot wait to see them this year.[33]

The Million-Dollar Mark

At home, Hannah and the Ladybug Foundation have raised more than $1.5 million for some 40 Canadian homeless shelters, food banks, and missions. The money is given to groups that touch a homeless person's life within 24 hours of receiving funds; places where people

Hannah visiting one of the shelters that the Ladybug Foundation financially supports.

live or take shelter; and places that feed homeless people or give food for such places.

Hannah has visited most of the shelters that the Ladybug Foundation supports. She points out that to be considered for funds, they must treat the people who come for help in a caring manner. "They all have an individual story. I meet them on the street. They say hello to me. They . . . have to talk to me first, so it is comfortable for both of us, and then I talk, and we get to know each other,"[34] Hannah says.

Hannah's parents are very proud of their daughter and amazed by some of the things she has accomplished. "Hannah whispers hope into everything,"[35] Colleen Taylor says. Those who know her best realize that where society sees a problem, Hannah sees a person. Colleen remembers one day in particular when her daughter was spending the afternoon at a homeless children's shelter in Toronto. Before leaving, Hannah hugged each child. A shy teen girl came to the front of the group and said to Hannah, "Until today I thought no one loved me, and now I know you do!"[36]

Chapter Four

A Message of Hope

For her hard work and dedication, Hannah has been the **recipient** of many honors. In 2007 she was a Brick Award winner in the category of Community Building. Do Something, a company that encourages young people to volunteer and get involved in the community, presents the award. That same year, the Women's Executive Network of Toronto named her as one of Canada's most powerful women. She was also asked to speak to an audience of 1,500 people at the award presentation.

Hannah is appreciative of such honors, but she says she feels a little funny inside about getting awards for doing what she knows in her heart is right. Still, the recognition is bringing her work to the attention of a wider audience. After the Brick Award ceremonies in New York, actress Hilary Swank offered to speak on Hannah's video. "If it means

Hannah was appreciative of actress Hilary Swank's offer to speak on a video Hannah was making to bring attention to homelessness.

more people will care and help the hungry and the homeless, then that is a good thing,"[37] Hannah says.

At the Ladybug Foundation

The Ladybug Foundation has many plans for the future. With Hannah as inspiration, the foundation has developed a national education project designed for schools from kindergarten through grade twelve. Hannah points out that she is just a regular kid who has had lots of opportunities to make her vision a reality. She would like to empower other children based on her experiences. The education project is a classroom program that includes music, software, books, and other great tools to help kids learn to "Make Change" in their world.

January 31, 2008, was the first annual Ladybug Foundation National Red Scarf Day. Hannah came up with the idea one frosty cold day as her mom wrapped a warm scarf around her neck. Thinking that many people do not have anything to keep out the cold, she decided to make cheerful red scarves with a message of caring and sell them. The proceeds go to help the homeless. The cozy scarves are available on the foundation's Web site during the coldest months of the year, from November to February. They are a popular item, and National Red Scarf Day was established so that thousands of people could wear them at the same time to show support for the homeless.

Hannah's Place

It is Hannah's hope that the day will come when no one has to sleep on the street or eat from the trash. That

Hannah puts her hand prints in the foundation of her new emergency homeless shelter called Hannah's Place. The shelter will offer food, showers, and beds for people who have no place else to go.

dream came one step closer to reality with the opening of Hannah's Place in May 2007. It is an emergency shelter where people can go for food, a shower, and a warm bed. It has a comfortable common lounge area, individual shower stalls, private changing rooms, and a place to do laundry.

The shelter is in Hannah's hometown of Winnipeg, where "there are 1,700 people living with no fixed address," says John Mohan, who runs the Siloam Mission. "During the first month that it was open it provided shelter to 274 people."[38] The shelter includes a section for men, one for young people, and one for women and children. "I was very honored to have it named after me," Hannah says. "I actually got to put my handprints in the cement and write my name in the cement."[39]

Ruby's Hope

When she was very young, Hannah sometimes worried that if she gave things away, she would have less. On December 1, 2007, she launched her first book, *Ruby's Hope*, a picture book that addresses that concern. Ruby is a young ladybug who learns that when you give from your heart, you get so much more in return. Hannah loved writing the book because she felt it was a great way to share her own feelings with younger children. "I am writing another book right now, but it is taking longer,"[40] she adds.

Hannah is no stranger to film either. The National Film Board of Canada followed her around for two years to **document** her life and work. The completed film is called *Hannah's Story*.

For the Future

Hannah's plans for the near future include working hard in school and traveling to serve on the children's jury in Sweden. She also hopes to visit an orphanage in Kenya and bring plenty of books for the library there.

In a few years, Hannah hopes to study at a university, but she is not certain about her final goal. She has considered becoming a dog breeder, an oceanographer, an archaeologist, a robotics engineer, or even the prime minister of Canada. She certainly hopes to write books and to be a mom. Most importantly, Hannah hopes to live in a world where everyone has shelter and food to eat.

Helping the Homeless

Hannah has plenty of suggestions for a young person who would like to help the homeless. She says the first

Hannah poses with her former first-grade teacher during a book signing for Hannah's first children's book titled *Ruby's Hope*.

thing to do is learn about the needs of the hungry and homeless in the community. Get in touch with local shelters, missions, and soup kitchens, and volunteer time and support.

Clothing, food, and toy drives are simple to organize in a neighborhood or school. Children can collect gently used clothing, shoes, and blankets from neighbors and donate them to missions and shelters.

Food banks always need canned goods, dry cereal, rice, and other foods that keep well. A school food drive may include a single class or the entire school. Some food banks accept homegrown produce in season, such as apples, pears, or peaches. Many charities collect new or used toys for homeless children, particularly during holiday seasons. Every donation, no matter how small, makes a difference.

Charities that help the homeless are always in need of money. Fund-raising is **critical** to keeping help available to those who need it. A young person who wants to collect donations can start by asking parents, teachers, and friends for ideas and for help.

There are plenty of methods to raise money for a good cause. Some traditional ways include a lemonade stand, a bake sale, or an art sale. There are less typical ways, too. One example is a sports day. Supporters pay each athlete for every mile they walk, run, ride, or swim.

Organizing a charity auction is a great way to encourage local businesses to help raise funds. Collect donations of goods such as movie tickets and restaurant meals or services such as a salon haircut or even babysitting. Invite friends and neighbors to bid on each donation.

One suggestion Hannah makes as a way people can help the homeless is to donate canned goods to a local food drive.

Even parties and dances may be opportunities to help the hungry and homeless. For a birthday party, create a wish list for charity. Ask friends and family to bring gifts of clothing or blankets for a local shelter. Have a school sock hop! Instead of tickets, make the entry fee three pairs of new socks per person that can be donated to a local shelter.

A Better Place

When asked why youngsters should care about the plight of people they do not know, Hannah is quick to reply: "We must care about each other and help and work together because it is our tomorrow, but it is also our today. When we care about each other, life is better for everyone. The world is better."[41]

Notes

Chapter One: A Kind Heart

1. Quoted in Ladybug Foundation, "Hannah's Letter to the Homeless." www.ladybugfoun dation.ca.
2. Hannah Taylor, interview with the author, October 26, 2007.
3. Hannah Taylor, interview.
4. Hannah Taylor, interview.
5. Hannah Taylor, interview.
6. Hannah Taylor, interview.
7. Hannah Taylor, interview.
8. Hannah Taylor, interview.
9. Quoted in How Stuff Works, "2007 BRICK Award Winner: Hannah Taylor." http:// people.howstuffworks.com/do-something -brick-awards-winner-hannah-taylor.htm.
10. Quoted in How Stuff Works, "2007 BRICK Award Winner."
11. Hannah Taylor, interview.

Chapter Two: Sad Hearts in Old Clothes

12. Quoted in My Hero, "Child Hero: Hannah Taylor, by Madison from Canada." www.my- hero. com/myhero/hero.asp?hero=htaylor_ canada_06.
13. Hannah Taylor, interview.

14. Hannah Taylor, interview.
15. Quoted in Ladybug Foundation, "Home." www.lady bugfoundation.ca.
16. Hannah Taylor, interview.
17. Hannah Taylor, interview.
18. Hannah Taylor, interview.
19. Hannah Taylor, interview.
20. Quoted in MTS Centre, "Northern Lights, Northern Stars," October 15, 2004. www.mtscentre.ca/press_releases/041015/index.php.
21. Hannah Taylor, interview.
22. Quoted in Tara Perkins, "Give a Little Love, Says Hannah," *Toronto Star*, November 23, 2006, p. C3.

Chapter Three: The Ladybug Foundation
23. Hannah Taylor, interview.
24. Lynda Horvath, interview with the author, December 4, 2007.
25. Quoted in Vancouver Dialogues, "On Nurturing Compassion & Educating the Heart," September 8, 2006. www.dalailamacenter.org/vancouverdialogues /2006/nurturing.php.
26. Quoted in Brainy Quote, "Martin Luther King, Jr. Quotes." www.brainyquote.com/quotes/authors/m/martin_luther_king_jr.html.
27. Hannah Taylor, interview.
28. Hannah Taylor, interview.
29. Hannah Taylor, interview.
30. Quoted in How Stuff Works, "2007 BRICK Award Winner."

31. Quoted in How Stuff Works, "2007 BRICK Award Winner."
32. Quoted in Gordon Sinclair, "Ladybug Girl Is Really Spreading Her Wings," *Winnipeg Free Press*, January 2007. www.winnipegfreepress.com/subscriber/colum nists/g_sinclair/story/3934445p-4546687c.html.
33. Hannah Taylor, interview.
34. Quoted in How Stuff Works, "2007 BRICK Award Winner."
35. Colleen Taylor, interview with author, October 26, 2007.
36. Colleen Taylor, interview.

Chapter Four: A Message of Hope

37. Hannah Taylor, interview.
38. Quoted in David Kuxhaus, "Homeless Shelter Celebrated," *Winnipeg Free Press*, June 30, 2007. www.winnipegfreepress.com/local/story/3998693p-4613559c.html.
39. Hannah Taylor, interview.
40. Hannah Taylor, interview.
41. Hannah Taylor, interview.

Glossary

charitable: Giving and helpful to others in need.

commitment: Devotion to a cause or duty.

compassionate: To be caring or understanding about the suffering of others.

conviction: A firm belief or opinion.

critical: Extremely important or serious.

debt slaves: People forced to work for nothing to pay off a debt.

dedication: Determination to work for a person or cause.

dignity: Self-respect, honor.

dilemma: A problem without a clear best solution.

disabilities: Conditions that make it difficult to perform daily activities.

disheveled: Untidy or disorderly.

document (verb): To make a record of something by writing it down or by taking a picture.

donor: Someone who gives something to another.

frustrated: Feeling annoyed and unsatisfied.

immigrants: People who move to a new country to live.

inspired: Encouraged or motivated to accomplish something.

jury: A select group of people who judge a competition.

patrons: People who support another person or thing.

persistent: Continuing in spite of problems.

plight: Difficulty; a sad and sometimes dangerous situation.

primatologist: A scientist who studies primates such as apes.

recipient: Someone who accepts or receives something.

refugees: People seeking safety or shelter from harm.

sponsorship: A pledge of money or help for a person or a cause.

tolerable: Acceptable.

For Further Exploration

Books

Margie Chalofsky, *Changing Places: A Kid's View of Shelter Living*. Mt. Rainier, MD: Gryphon House, 1992. Eight homeless children, ages six to thirteen, tell stories about what it is like to be homeless and living in a shelter.

Lindsay Lee Johnson, *Soul Moon Soup*. Asheville, NC: Front Street, 2002. After her father deserts them, Phoebe Rose and her mother are homeless. Their lives become a struggle that they must face every day. The story is told in verse.

Cathryn Berger Kaye, *A Kids' Guide to Hunger & Homelessness: How to Take Action!* Camden, MN: ABCD Books, 2007. A student workbook that helps children learn about the causes and effects of hunger and homelessness. It includes information on how to start a service project.

Hannah Taylor, *Ruby's Hope*. Winnipeg, Canada: The Ladybug Foundation Education Program, 2007. In this picture book, a young ladybug sees a homeless bumblebee and wants to help.

Maria Testa, *Someplace to Go*. Morton Grove, IL: Albert Whitman, 1996. In this picture book, most of the students go home after school, but not Davey. He is homeless. He and his mother and brother sleep at a shelter and eat at a soup kitchen.

Web Sites

Do Something.org (www.dosomething.org). This site is designed to help young people get involved in their global and local communities. The site offers ideas for projects and fund-raising, tips on getting grants, and other ways to get the word out about a worthy cause. Children and teens can also join the Do Something Club or participate in current drives to fight hunger and world poverty.

JustGive.org (www.justgive.org/html/ways/fundraise. html). A nonprofit organization designed to connect people with many types of charities and causes. It gives ideas for fund-raising, facts about donating, inspirational quotes, and more. It offers advice especially for children.

The Ladybug Foundation (www.ladybugfoundation.ca). Go to this site to keep up with news about Hannah Taylor and the Ladybug Foundation. It includes information about homelessness and special "Kids Only" and "You Can Help" sections.

The My Hero Project (www.myhero.com/myhero/ home. asp). A site created by teachers for teachers and students. Young people can read and write about their heroes. The site includes many different categories, such as human rights heroes, peacemakers, and child heroes.

World's Children's Prize for the Rights of the Child (www.childrensworld.org). The site explains that the

World's Children's Prize for the Rights of the Child "empowers young people so that they can make their voices heard and demand respect for their rights." The site gives information on activists for the rights of children, how to become a global friend, and how children everywhere can support the rights of children.

Index

A
Adams, Rick, 13–14

B
Brick Award for Community Building, 4, 28

F
Fund-raising
   Hannah's efforts at, 14–15
   importance of, 34
   by Ladybug Foundation, 20, 26–27

G
Goodall, Jane, 23

H
Hannah's Place, 30–31
Hannah's Story (film), 32
Harper, Stephen, 23

Homeless/homelessness
   Hannah becomes concerned with, 8–10
   reasons for, 11–12
   ways children can help, 34–35
Horvath, Linda, 21

K
King, Martin Luther, Jr., 21–22
Kreviazuk, Chantal, 16

L
Ladybug Foundation, 4
   on changes in homeless population, 11
   establishment of, 19
   fund-raising by, 20, 26–27
   future plans of, 30

Hannah as voice of,
20–21, 22–23
roots of, 15–16
Ladybug Foundation National Red Scarf Day, 30

M
Make Change Month, 16
Martin, Paul, 23
Mohan, John, 31

N
National Film Board of
Canada, 32

R
Ruby's Hope (Hannah
Taylor), 32

S
St. John's-Ravenscourt
School, 7–8
Swank, Hillary, 28–29

T
Taylor, Bruce (father), 5
Taylor, Colleen (mother),
5, 16, 23, 27

Taylor, Hannah Catherine
awards won by, 4, 28
becomes concerned with
homelessness, 8–10
birth of, 5
fund-raising by, 14–15
future plans of, 33
as juror for World's
Children Prize, 25
meets with business
leaders, 16–18
pastimes of, 7
sources of inspiration
for, 21–22
typical schedule of,
23–24
on ways children
can help homeless,
34–36
Taylor family, 5–7

W
Women's Executive
Network of Toronto,
28
World's Children Prize
for Rights of the Child,
25

Picture Credits

About the Author

Q.L. Pearce has written more than one hundred trade books for children and more than thirty classroom workbooks and teacher manuals on the topics of reading, science, math, and values. Pearce has written science-related articles for magazines; regularly gives presentations at schools, bookstores, and libraries; and is a frequent contributor to the educational program of the Los Angeles County Fair. She is the assistant regional adviser for the Society of Children's Book Writers and Illustrators in Orange, San Bernardino, and Riverside counties and is a member of the advisory board for Writing for Children program at the California State University at Fullerton.